# Bones of Birds

# Bones of Birds

Jo Colley

Smokestack Books
1 Lake Terrace, Grewelthorpe, Ripon HG4 3BU
e-mail: info@smokestack-books.co.uk
www.smokestack-books.co.uk

ISBN 978-0-9929581-1-4

Middlesbrough
moving forward

Smokestack Books is
represented by Inpress Ltd

To GW
'Never tell the one you love that you do
Save it for the deathbed'
*'Cardinal Song', The National*

# Contents

# old ladies have the bones of birds

portmanteau oxygen
                    secrete breath
make space to travel light
leave this world with a gentle shove
from shoe rejecting feet
                    take flight
the distant sky they gazed at
from flat on their backs
now their milieu
                    the bleu

enter their designated realm
                    little witches
of skies and trees
wonder workers
the birch between
                    their legs

with what relief they cast off
                    the foot binds
the apron strings
the ties that tethered
jettison pies, irons, plans,
                            photos
released balloons
        the gentle drift
                    up up and away
their day
            come at last

# Crows

slow circle the beech,
a séance,
a synchronised return

to matchstick cities where
they perch and preen,
replete with scraps.

Sky pirates, poised
for aerial display
or sudden flight.

Boot polished heads,
slick feathers,
the scalloped fan of outstretched wings.

In courtly trios
you flaunt your risky glamour.
I would ride you if I could.

# Piecework

Cornflower eyes still sharp enough
to thread a needle, and the hands,
age hennaed, keep stitching
as the sunlight fades.

At 13 you took the bus up west
from Hornsey Rise to Bond Street,
found a poorly paid position
in a sweat shop piecing furs.

You sewed your own wedding:
wartime coupons stretched to fit.
Three kids: a set of fifties mannequins
for home-made shirts and Hilda's knits.

From treadle to the latest in electric
you've zigzagged twice around the world,
transformed cloth into creation:
tucked, pinned, thimbled, spooled.

As a child, your mother working,
minded by Aunt Lot in Duncan Road
you taught yourself to play her upright
by writing all the letters on the keys.

You shivered in that chilly parlour,
frozen fingers poised, as your mind
combined notes, like colours, made shapes
that hovered for a second, then were gone.

# Heiress

Her little finger trapped in a car door
when she was three years old,
stained the beige suede
of the customised Bentley,
evoking her father's disgust.

The mangled digit, preserved in formaldehyde
became her loyal companion, one step up
from an imaginary friend.
Its messages were indirect: ask it a question
and it would turn slowly
revolving in its pickle jar like a mutant fish
until it settled in a particular direction.

Sometimes she took this as a no,
Sometimes a yes.

When more intricate advice was called for
she'd remove the lid, insert one perfect hand,
grasp the squirming thing like a flesh pencil,
dip it in ink. Let it write instructions
on an A3 sheet. All advice, she followed
to the letter: homework, helpful hints
on how to dress. What strategies
can mend a broken heart.

Her mother's disappearance was a mystery.
Although there was no love lost, still
she felt the need to settle her unease.
The accusing finger showed her where
the evidence was buried and who
had mud on his boots. Her father

took the clichéd course, with
some assistance on the trigger.
Now all is well. They winter in St Lucia,
spend the summers motoring abroad.
She drives the Bentley, whilst her companion
map reads, indicates the finest of the views.

# Mrs Robinson's dress

In Redcar Oxfam, I uncover the dress,
hold my breath as I take it to the till,
unable to relax until it's mine. In the car,
it sings to me like Ulysses, tells its traveller's tale.

Oyster moygashel, silk lined in palest pink
only a pearl would dare to insert itself
into that world. Mrs Robinson: her lighthouse beam
ignites every dollared pageant of Los Angeles.

So tall in her stilettos, she can see clear across
the top of her husband's balding head,
his thick specs level with her breasts,
cone shaped, straining the stretched fabric.

She locks double-lashed eyes with Benjamin,
tender as a new born rabbit. The dress
beckons him into her bed, his clumsy hands
caught on its hook, lost in its eye.

Later, sated, she dumps it in the trash.
Her maid retrieves it, gives it closet space
until her oldest son comes out, his drag act,
a revelation from port to shining port,

gains him access to the captain's table,
the first mate's bed. Until, on Teesside,
he jumps ship, sheds the dress. His loss,
my gain. So here's to you, Mrs Robinson.

# Dorothy

That last week, I picked
six perfect strawberries
from the allotment,
hulled them with a scalpel
put them in a white porcelain bowl,
brought them to your bed.
Your face, turned primate, yellow
as a page from an ancient book,
looked at them with the shadow
of appetite. I put them in your hand.
You ate them, taking your time.
The seeds went with you
back into the earth.

# Joyce

Neat as a new pin in tailored slacks
striped top, and cotton cardigan,
standing up to her 80 odd years
tall and straight. Bullet proof,
she shields herself from questions
that fall like arrows from the sky.

All around, a twitter of gossip: why
do her sisters never visit? who
was the woman at her husband's funeral,
the boy who held her hand? why
is noone ever asked across
the threshold of her curtained door?

She never shed a public tear:
what happens behind the nets
is her affair, and her affair alone.
People forget she was a top PA
to an architect in Regents Street,
never beautiful (the nose too big)
but always perfectly groomed.

Just lately, a neighbour's tree roots
have wormed their way into
her foundations. She won't move.
She has, in her drawer, under
the paired up gloves, a little box of pills.
She'll know when the time has come
to swallow, swallow, swallow.

## Wren haiku

Find a wren's feather
on the way to your wedding
wear it in your hair.

They say she's the bride
of Cock Robin. He offers
the warmth of his breast.

On St Stephen's day
she must strive to hold her tongue:
some folk want her dead.

# Air hostess

Back then, it was different: us girls aspired
to serve. Miles high in polyester pencil skirt,
our taut thighs held in sheerest nylon
a nifty cap perched on hair sprayed stiff as wire.

Solicitous, skin pancaked to perfection,
we soothed the weary men, always ready
with lighter, ice and paper bag. Up there, heads
hollowed out by butane, we communicated clink and fizz.

Just in time, my unwavering lipstick smile
bagged me my BOAC man. Grounded at 30,
with a new life in the Cotswolds, I've adjusted.
Turbulence is rare. I tend my garden, planted

in neat rows, like the seats in business class.
The flowers lift their faces as I pass.

# The best possible thing

'Flying is the best possible thing for women'
*Elise Deroche, first woman to fly solo 1910*

# Amy Johnson's Pigskin Bag

Secure in your glass case like Snow White
in no danger of an awakening kiss,
everything you know contained.

Your thick skin resists the January sea.
You bob above the waves, whistle
a shanty, as she strives,

then slips beneath the ship's stern.
Time on your side, you float, oblivious,
as another weaker vessel sinks.

Sole survivor, you let yourself
be hauled on deck, move on to glory.
All her journeys hidden

in your unreflective maw.
You keep it zipped, lolling tongue
firmly held in your pig's cheek.

## Lady Drummond-Hay:
## From Lakehurst to Friedrichshaven

Invited to dance as the ragtime plays,
the whole world elevated from the mud
and up, up in the air. She grabs
the proffered hand of fate, lifts off
in a cathedral, its filigree arches
supporting straining silk, like
a generous woman in a corset.

Dangled in a gondola, her eyes devour
the Zeppelin's shadow, a giant cigar
drifting over the surface of the earth.
A series of tableaux: mountains,
sunlit seas, the sculpted desert floor,
empty plains that stretch forever,
cities built from a child's wooden blocks.

The airship is a silent ghost, hovering,
and she a benign deity, a sole goddess
among the handpicked, hardened hacks,
hers the only news in town. Her words
fall from the sky like revelations. Before
she lands, she jettisons her heart,
its weight a burden she can live without.

# Amelia Earhart's Little Red Bus

*Museum of Air and Space, Washington, May 2011*

All week, the heat of new summer, against
the dark rain-heavy skies , thunder rumbles,
spreads unease. Today, skies flag blue,
people drink iced sodas outside cafes,
the city loosens its belt. Unruly kids
in coloured polo shirts roam in packs,
click digitals in front of history,
missing the point. Humble, I stand before
the little red bus. Your cardboard figure
leans, gazing back: the disguising fringe falls
towards a shy smile, a wide mouth divides
the flat plains of your face. I've crossed an ocean
to be here, to see the bus, flamboyant, lipstick red
its cheerful glamour refusing to fade.
On a distant atoll in another dimension,
your American bones and teeth
bleach white beneath the sand.

# Garbo of the Skies

*Jean Batten born
New Zealand 1909,
died Majorca 1982*

# Portent, Rotorura 1912

Jean could leave her presence in the room
and vanish, so you didn't notice
that she'd gone. A trick she practised
until perfect. There we were, her brothers,

by the window, watching the thunder,
the sheeting rain, lightning zigzag down.
There she was, out in the yard, curls
straightening with the weight of water,

dropped teddy drowning at her feet.
Gazing at the sky as if the clouds
might come to fetch her: winged horses,
a chariot of fire.

# Mother's milk

First she cleared the nest.
Removed each boy child
with her ruthless beak.
Each night, she returned,
puked the day's kill
straight into my gullet.
Made me swallow, gagging,
force fed me til I sprouted
feathers for my own flight.

# Mother attends Open Day at the Ladies College

If all your friends have mothers like mice,
dressed in gentle shades of brown,
your own, hawk-eyed, with a wing span
like an eagle's, is dramatic.

When she comes, the wind shifts,
lifts the hair on the back of your head.
You try to hide yourself among
the brown skirts, quivering.

She swoops down, triumphant,
a fox pelt draped around her neck.
She claims you for her chick.

# Compass

Where North Island's waist
is slim enough for a man's hands
to encompass, I learn the art
of getting lost. The little pointer spins,
uncertain, the coloured maps
are mysteries. Then Dad shows me
how to set the needle,
translate the contours into paths,
use an instinct for direction
to show us our way home.

Later after everything has shifted
and I've drifted off the course we set,
I hear him calling. Just once,
then everything goes quiet.

# Advice

When the engine suddenly spluttered
then stopped. The whine that had
accompanied her for hours gone silent
like a tired child giving in to sleep.
When the exhausted bird drifted
towards the water and she could not
urge it into life, she thought of Smithy.
'You'll need a revolver – if there's sharks.
To shoot yourself.'

In her hand the one inch picture
Bader gave her. 'Look for the palm trees.
Let the lighthouse guide you down.'

# Flying blind

You're caught for hours in a grey bubble
somewhere between sea and sky, unsure
which way is up. Your blistered hand
pumps fuel into the tank until it bleeds.
The compass is all you have.

Then the needle wavers, spins around,
points back the way you've come.
Flying blind, you feel your way through vapour.
Just the ghost of where you think
you're going, the hope of solid earth.

# Inspiration

She swings the propeller, takes off
in her Gipsy Moth, goggles down,
the helmet tight around her ears.

Her hawk-eyed mother follows her
across the skies cackling encouragement
louder than the engine's whine.

Her father, far below, swings his golf club.
The ball flies way across the clouds
lands in his daughter's lap.

They do not weigh her down nor alter
the course she plotted for herself. For days
and days she is alone in that small space

dissecting the sky. She looks down
on miniature cities, fields no bigger
than a thumbnail, oceans misting out of sight.

Clouds and sea lift invisible hands,
transport her through the grey, regal,
like a little empress on a velvet cushion.

# Final flight

She wanders the gardens of Palma, earthbound
without the compass of her mother's presence,
the skies, her former playground, no longer blue.
She begins her laborious descent,
sees Rotorura in the rain swept view.
Wings clipped, her eyes on the ground
she wanders the gardens of Palma, earthbound,
until disguised as a dog, opportunity bites.
She prepares herself for her final flight.
The gardens recede. No longer earthbound.

# The Night Witches:
# Russian fliers 1942-1946

# Nachthexen

If there's a bomber's moon
we make our calls. The two of us
like lovers, prepare careful gifts,

negotiate the wind's direction,
manipulate our battered craft,
no better than a broomstick.

Through the dark, our cat's eyes
open up the night, home in
on where the boys are

fighting to stay awake.
We're quiet as we approach
like anxious mothers tiptoeing,

let our engines idle to glide
light as goose down til we feel
their warm breath on our cheeks.

Their faces change like children
in a nightmare as they realise
why we've come. They struggle

to unravel from their beds,
run for cover as we offer them
our gifts of fire, of sleep.

# Polikarpov P0-2

Plodding like a plough horse,
the plane carries her,
belly skimming fields and farms
to where the boys sleep,
dreaming of girls with flaxen hair
and breasts like pillows,
of Mutti and her mixing bowl
and all the warmth of home.

She switches off the engine, becomes
a bi-winged moth, soft in the moonlight.
Wafts down on a breath of wind,
lets loose her presents, one,
then two. They flower like carnations
as she makes her turn, retraces
the flight path, trailing
proud banners of smoke.

# Tidying up

So many missions, sooner or later,
I knew I would be hit. When the moment came
I had to look for a way through,
something I could do
to save the situation. Going down,
skin stretched hard over bone,
my life as a cartoon flashing by,
I drew myself a door. Saw

an empty frame just beyond
the forest, willed myself to land.
I felt proud that day, stepping away
from our battered bird, all three of us
alive. Behind us, the burning wreck
of another plane, upended in the trees.
Those boys thought they were gods.

We found what we could of them,
an arm, a leg, smouldering remains.
Not a single head. Buried them there.
Our parachutes their shrouds.

# The smell of petrol

Fuel was pouring from our engine
flames gaining ground. Even now,
I don't know how Yekaterina

brought us down, just behind our lines.
I was drunk on the vapour from the fuel,
staggering about with my axe

whilst the two of them cursed me,
screaming, trapped in the cockpit.
God knows where I found the strength

to get them out before the thing went up.
But do you know, as we lay there
on the blessed earth, some infantry lads

crawled up to find us. They brought us
strawberries, huge and ripe,
resplendent on a dish of leaves.

I can see them now. The green and the red.

# Lydia Vladimirovna Litvyak (Lylia)
# Russian Ace 1922-1943

*Lylia refuses to cut her hair*

No matter what you offer – your life
your youth – the great machine wants more.
I did not understand why I had to
cut my hair, offer up my curls
in sacrifice when they had all the rest.
Vanity perhaps. I wanted to see
my own face in the mirror each day
before I took off. Besides, it's cold
up there! Where's the harm in hair?
They forced me to conform,
but never knew, I stole peroxide
from the hospital. What hair I had
was going to stay blonde.

# Marina Raskova Disciplines Lylia

I'd heard she was one of our best recruits,
a daring flier with a cool head. On her first parade,
I noticed she had trimmed the fur from her boots
to make a collar. Her fox face peaked out cheekily.

I hardened my heart. 'When did you do this?'
I asked, sterner than Comrade Stalin.
She needed to know who was in charge.
Maybe I was unsure myself, scarcely older

than she. 'In the night, Comrade Major,'
she told me, half defiant, half dismayed.
She was a creature from a fairy tale,
cutting and stitching, an elf intent

on transforming the dull cloth to preserve
her femininity, outshine the other girls.
To think she would squander her sleep,
sit up until dawn for the sake of fashion.

I sent her to the isolation cell,
made her sacrifice another night,
unpick each stitch, replace the fur
on her boots. By God that girl could fly.

# Lilya Looks Back

I was so young: I didn't know
what it was to be afraid. Lying
on my back in summer grass,
long before the war clouds gathered.
the sky called me: my element,
more bird than girl.

The Nazis came, darkened the sun
like a flock of crows. I made myself eagle,
clenched my tender heart into a fist,
watched bullets stitch a perfect seam
through the blue to undo the cocky boys,
fine examples of the master race.

Even as I watched my sisters die,
melt like candles in their Yaks,
I felt alive. Our days were short
but we made them long: each night
ended in song, our girls' voices
offered to the stars.

Like Baba Yaga, I covered my tracks,
swept away all traces, left them wondering.
The lily painted on my side beguiled them
as I unleashed a rain of burning petals.
Dressed to kill, I led them in a dance
more intimate than love.

Now and then, drifting home,
dawn colouring my cheeks,
I would recall a night before the war
swaying to a jazz band, a boy I hardly knew.
His hands on the small of my back,
my face against his chest.

In the end, I didn't see them coming.
I was tired, and the sun was in my eyes.
They tore at me like a pack of dogs,
ripped away a wing. I spiralled down to earth,
bid my mother goodbye.
Such noise, such pain. Then silence.

But here I sit, a grandma in a tidy German garden,
my white hair carefully arranged, cheeks like wrinkled apples.
The broken bones mended, though they feel the cold.
I had to seal the jar to my past
with a good thick layer of wax
to make this trade: my country for my life.

Only the sky knows no boundaries.

# Medals

Her left breast supports
a heavy row of medals.
He wonders if she's cut it off,
an Amazonian gesture
to make room for more.

Or if he were to open up
her shirt, he'd find
breasts cone-shaped as shells
with nipples like red stars.

# Standing By

# The night my father turned into a tree

*i.m Lancaster LM631 207 Squadron*
*Thursday 27 April 1944*

From that other plane the men dropped like dolls
were found by village boys strung in the trees,
fire-singed puppets, parachutes half-opened,
Rolls Royce engines scattered on the forest floor.

Muir, Loveday, Collins
Fawcett, Buxton, Upsall,
Longmate. Their fates entangled,
fused in one searing moment.

He spiralled out, landed in the pines
sat quiet for a while, gathering himself,
not thinking of the others, where they were
whilst the pilotless plane hit the Hohloh.

That night, my father turned into a tree,
wrapped himself in bark thick enough
to prepare him for all he had to do
to survive dark days in cold camps,

walk frozen miles to the girl who waited,
blind to the transformation. She
nested in his complicated branches,
sat tight as the rot devoured him.

Jones, Seibel, Exley,
Ignanni, Carmichael, Griffin,
Watts.

Metal fragments, like pieces of a scattered star,
carbonated, wait to be found by a German boy
whose mother, as a girl, saw Ray Watts' body
laid in the village churchyard.

My daughter and I stand with the German boy
in the cold wet morning, among the stunted trees,
honour the ground where the plane hit,
listen to the wind, nothing but the wind.

# Gravity

A haze of wedding veil drifts far above,
star sprinkled through this summer night,
trailing beauty to the sigh of the sea.

My neck hurts as I try to angle
the heavy garden seat planted square
on the flat surface of the Suffolk earth.

I remember the paper balloons you used to make:
lit inside with a resolute flame,
they rose and rose then vanished into space.

It was before I knew about the jump
to save your life, the drift through the dark,
the parachute above you, diaphanous as smoke.

This morning, the swallows circle the house.
Butterflies attend a flower feast:
honeysuckle, lavender, buddleia, rose.

Each year I'm heavier, more rooted to the earth.
The chicken daughter of an eagle and a wren,
wings clipped, I dream of falling into the blue.

## Stanley Crescent 1969

You rise up like Persephone, blinking
from the dark basement, sit on the steps
of the wedding cake house to read the letter.

It's slim, crisp as a new note, trimmed
with promise. An unknown president
regards you from its stamp.

You sit, beatific as Buddha, the letter
in your lap, blue and white London light
swirling like a day at the beach.

All week you have waited, standing
in the ominous hallway, ears straining
for the postman's footsteps.

Your fingers tear along the dotted line,
release a sigh of longing from the slanting script,
the curling down strokes.

Passing pigeons circle as your heart
war dances round the fire, smoke rising
like an exhaled breath spells 'yes.'

# Witness

I lived below ground, but
the sun found me, pushing
through the bars of my window
to light up the poster of Dylan
that almost covered one wall.

Living my fictional life in the city
still inside my small town skin,
I felt it stretch, begin to split
along the stitched up seams
as the heat of summer deepened.

Each Friday, you knocked on my door
and I drifted through the hall
like a released dandelion seed,
carrying all I might become
into the warm circle of your arms.

One Sunday morning, all my stitches
came undone. Bob looked on
as tender new wings unfurled.
Under the pillow, two tickets
for the Isle of Wight.

# Comrades

You and me, a mattress on the floor
and the old Soviet Union map
guarding one wall. Before and after,
I would stare at the expanse
try the place names in my head:
the romance of otherness,
letters back to front or altogether different.
We made love like comrades
to the Red Army Choir.

You tried to learn the language,
listened to the tapes and practised for a while.
I liked the way your lips looked
when you said Spacebo and Niet.
We said we'd go there one day
take a steamship down the Volga
eat Red October chocolate
wearing our authentic Russian hats.

Glasnost was our downfall. You were gutted
as all across the map borders surfaced.
The reversal turned your whole world upside down.
Paranoid as Stalin, you dispatched me to the gulag
for crimes against the state, rewrote our history
with my image airbrushed out. Now you're holed up
in the dacha, hoarding resentment like a kulak
while I rub my mittened fingers in the cold.

# Into the redwoods brooding

The blurred heart still visible on the trunk
of the veteran beech in Brusselton Woods
as it sprouts new leaves like green mayday flags
ahead of the tardy bluebells
I take as a good sign. Years ago
in another wood, consumed by flames,
I melted like a candle. Lost my shape,
no longer fitted for the life that waited.

This woman, patient in her old coat
is content to stand, watch the blue tits
mate mid air above the fallen oak,
its roots visible like arteries in a post mortem.
I lean against it, feel its uneven skin.
You fill sacks with leaf mould,
your hands inside the earth
coaxing the rich clods to the surface.

As we make our way back to the car,
we inhale the forest smells, crouch
to catch the perfume of a primrose
see wood anemones nod pale heads
the breeze still chill after this long winter.
I hold your muddy hand, drawing its warmth,
feel the blood pump
through the veins in your wrist.

## No Woman No Cry 1979

My sky high consciousness spins me
into orbit, and the air is Thatcher blue.
You are at your most new man handsome:
the women form an orderly queue.
You receive them in the Tyneside flat
flanked by bookend toms, their balls intact.
I am Laika, howling space dog in the manger
looking down from long dead eyes
to see you walk a woman home.
I soak myself in gin like a sloe
but the bitterness persists.
Sometimes we dance together
to ska or reggae for the brotherhood of man.
I learn what it means to remove
your own skin and find nothing underneath.

# Fungi

Field mushrooms:
flat white dinner plates
stud the verges
under a turning beech.

A penny bun squats
boletus edulis
its domed head glistens
like buttered toast.

Earth balls erupt
In pustulent profusion.
Squeeze gently: repopulate
the world.

# Pairings

In the silent evening, we come upon
three cygnets, almost grown, white
displacing brown. They slow glide
across the pond's surface,
cartoon feet hard at work,
though they seem to be drawn
by an invisible cord.

*In Regent's Park, under a tree, you*
*in a paisley shirt, me in Bus Stop crepe.*
*The future cracks the mirrored surface*
*of the lake, waves its two-edged sword.*

Displayed like slaves at auction,
the young show each side
to best advantage whilst
the mated pair attend: steady, careworn
with a frailty under the white plumes
that suggests a sense of duty:
Once joined, they can't be free.

Not even with those wings. That beauty.

# Dub Be Good To Me 1989

On a Brittany beach I read my book,
look up from time to time
to watch you in the water
with our daughters.
Their striped bathers dip
in and out of the waves,
illustrate the life of Riley
as the sea glitters endlessly
and I believe I will be happy
for the rest of my life.

This is holiday: you are released,
light as the kites you fly,
beyond the rub a dub of day to day
the man who only leaves his box
when summer comes. A short spell
in the sun then back to the shadows:
a condemned man whose sentence
rules us all.

That cool September day,
when you held out your hand
to take me down, I turned away.

# My Father's Tankard

'Look into the pewter pot
To see the world as the world's not.'
*A.E. Housman*


Start with the base metal,
find it wanting: too soft
to be of any use. Add
antimony, bismuth, copper,
zinc or lead, for extra weight.
Planish to an understated grey,
fashion a vessel consummately plain,
the surface just catching
the bar's low light. Your life
reflected, hazy and unclear.
The more you drain it,
the less I see of you.

**Slip stream**

# View from a bridge

The skiff splits the river's skin
makes it bleed into geometry,
leaving patterned ripples
that fade like frowns.

Eyes ahead, she calculates the angles
to keep her clear of fallen branches,
maintains her poise around each turn,
light as a leaf.

She reads the water's hexagrams,
includes her body's mathematics,
calibrates the breeze
that lifts her hair.

Her long white legs extend,
a balance for the endless oars
she works with wrists that cross
and flex. Oblique, single, she powers on.

My eyes strain to keep her
as she disappears from view.
I watch until all trace of her
has gone.

## Après moi

That weekend, the north west sky
opened on us like a bible:
lakes puddled round our knees,
downpours mocked the gortex,
a deluge showed us
we were less than watertight.

The sky cried for us: all
the stored up tears of decades
burst through that heroic membrane,
like when the ceiling fell on us
when we were young and strong.

The rain seems drier now. My raincoat
hangs forlorn, wellingtons unworn
for years. I look at my hands.
The skin is cracking like the desert floor.

# Precipitation

Through the rain pearled window of the Starbucks
outside Embankment Tube, I see you come,
long legs high stepping through your day to mine.

Everything stops to look at you – taxis,
tourists, pigeons, raindrops – all
swirl into a rapturous blur. You,

your blue eyes electrify
the coffee sipping corporates as you
stoop to shake the diamonds from your hair.

Oh so short a time, minutes to be here,
drink you in with a small Americano,
see your perfect hands pull apart a muffin.

Whilst you offer me crumbs of information
from the banquet of your life, I try
to lock you up and throw away the key,

shrink you to pocket size,
ignore the protest of your lashes
against the prison of my palm.

Outside the gallery
you kiss my cheek goodbye,
direct me to Leicester Square.

I lived here once.

# Lamb

I emerge from the sweaty heaving underground
like a slippery newborn spilled into life,
stop to call you in the exhaled breath of coffee
and Millie's Cookies but you've switched off.
Out on Lower Marsh the rain begins to fall:
I think about going back to buy an umbrella,
then I remember I have never had
a long-term relationship with an umbrella
only infrequent, desperate one night stands
with no commitment on either side.

Near Waterloo the railway legacy
leaves scattered viaducts, lost cathedrals.
Sheltered here, waiting for the rain to pause,
where mutant pigeons drink from rainbowed puddles,
the city reveals a secret: Blake's Songs,
transposed to mosaic, each tiny piece of coloured clay
arranged to make a perfect copy of the book
you gave me when innocence outweighed experience.

# Lucky

In 1973 you crept across the Tyne
the collar of your flimsy London coat
turned up against the wind
chilblains on your gloveless hands.
You'd ended up on the wrong side
of the wrong river. It made you cry.

Decades and many bridges later,
when the wrong side flipped
like a coin suddenly turned lucky,
layered in years against the cold
you point your Yoko torch across the water
at fancy flats and franchised bars

signal as instructed:
dah … dah dah …. dahdahdah
I ….love…you.
I ….love …you.

# Night vision

You take the plunge: everything
submerged except your stubborn head,
up to your neck in it. Eye to eye
with the water's skin, its skittered surface
restless, like fingers, drumming on a bar,
summoning percussive thoughts
that patter up your spine.

Down you go to join your demons,
surrender to the dark, the ebb and flow,
use flippered feet to make your way
to her untidy bed. Search with fingertips
for clues, like a blind man tracing
his wife's face to check that she is true.
Encounter nothing that's conclusive.

Stay down as long as you can manage:
listen to the echo of your breath
deduce the origins of objects
barnacled in failure and regret.
But in the end your cylinder begins
the apprehensive cough of nearing empty.
You kick out for the light.

# Alnmouth, October

Under a big sky soft as a pigeon's wing,
the colours of Northumberland merge:
pearl grey, oyster, sand,
the blue black rippled sea
run together like water spilled on a child's painting,
a perfect marbled sheet, enfolding us like gift wrap.

My body chooses baptism
emerges from the water
in obedience to moon and tide.

A seismic planetary shift
has exhumed all lost days
resurrected from a black hole.
They erupt onto the beach, reborn
like corpses in a Stanley Spencer churchyard,
scattered offerings brought into the light.

I stand before you in the sweet, salt air
a message hidden in a bottle
you must break open to read.

The dark line of rocks rises into cormorant
as gulls cast wave shaped shadows on sand
carved by the retreating tide.
My hand hides in your hand,
our Siamese skin stitched together
like a boy and his shadow.

## Siren

She was working as a mermaid
in an 80s bar, not far from the waterfront.
I watched in wonder as her buoyant breasts

broke surface through the white stream
of her hair. She slipped out of her fish tail
a pearl abandoning an oyster

a sailor's wet dream.
I took her home, suppressed the urge
to run the bath. Felt her real legs

wrap around me like weeds
believed she would stay,
moored to my delusions.

She learned to poledance whilst
my back was turned. Twizzled
like a schoolgirl in the park,

coiled herself around the nearest
better offer, leaving me
high and dry.

Today, I'm on the river, taking sounds
plumbing the depths
cold as a fish on a slab.

# River Goddess

These arms (my best feature) broad as hams
have heaved me up and down this stretch
for centuries. The tail helps, of course:
gets you out of trouble with a well-timed flip

keeps boats at bay. My troutskin bra's
a legend among anglers. Some swear
they've seen me, boast about my breasts
extend their lying palms.

Once, or maybe twice, I've taken one.
Knocked him off his piddling stool into my reach
shown him a fin or two, then thrown him back.
Tell that to your mates, I say, and laugh.

# Salvage

*Items commemorating the wreck of the SS Stanley on 23 November 1864 on the Black Middens at Tynemouth, Tyne and Wear*

## I      Cutlery

The cutlery, displayed on white, is a chorus line
the bowl of each tarnished spoon glinting
like a face turning to the light.

The knives are mini scimitars, embossed with rolls
and curls, homage to the sea they were fished from
all those years ago

The girls were found on Mussell Scarp
their linen swaddled bodies
laid out in the morgue, side by side.

## II      John Sopwith's dictionary

Words and their definitions cannot be erased.
No storm can silence such a store
so carefully compiled.

The sea added salt. The printed pages
washed up on the beach survived.
Choose. Write your epitaphs.

## III      Wallace Gravestone

Salt and wind eat stone
eradicate the message
meant to last forever.

Underneath, the bones
settle in their bed of soil
knowing who they are.

# Peg Powler

Mothers use my name to scare their children
I don't object. I have none of my own
but understand the depth of the seduction
the way the mirrored surface draws you down.

They say I scatter trinkets to entice them
bright fairings twinkling on the banks
just close enough to deeper waters where
the fickle currents spin you til you drown.

I'm misrepresented. The mothers
need the clout of magic to colour in
what might have been an empty threat
I'd do the same. But hear me.

We do not ask for sacrifice, nor
lure tots into our waiting arms.
If they fall, we hold them gently,
rock them til the final bubble

leaves the infant mouth, floats up
and breaks the surface carrying
that last mama to ears that strain
but never hear it. Just the river rolling by.

# Mum's call, 18 Jan 2010

Today she believes she left her bed
travelled up to Hull
knocked on Kath's door
to have that conversation about
why Ron hanged himself.

She wants to know, was it
his failing sight, the Hopper curse?
She could have helped him
told him about her second
corneal graft, given him hope

he would not fall into the dark.
Or was it, as Alma thinks, that
Kath was having an affair
and Ron couldn't stand it,
not after what Joey did to him

during the war. 'So what did Kath say?'
I ask her, intrigued at where
her fancy takes her. 'She didn't say.
But not his eyes, she thinks.
Not his eyes.'

# Acknowledgements

'Into the redwoods brooding' was first published in *By Grand Central Station I Sat Down and Wept* (Red Squirrel Press, 2010); 'Heiress' and 'Siren' were published by *Kumquat Poetry* in 2013.

I would like to thank Angela Readman for her insight, clarity, and sharp-eyed editing, Lisa Matthews for the joy of Poetry Heads, Kirsten Luckins from Apples and Snakes and all the women from the Tees Valley Rehearsal Group for their love and support.